Great Names in History

BENJAMIN FRANKLIN

by Patricia Green

illustrated by
Ghislaine Joos

HART-DAVIS

Benjamin Franklin was born on January 17th 1706 in Boston in America, at the sign of the Blue Ball in Milk Street. His father was a soap-maker and candle-maker. In those days very large families were common and Benjamin was one of seventeen children, though not all of them survived to grow up. But Benjamin was a sturdy child, and when he was eight his father sent him to Boston Grammar School. Probably his mother had already taught him to read because Benjamin himself tells us that 'I do not remember a time when I could not read'. He stayed less than a year at the Grammar School and was sent to another school for a further year. Then he left school for ever. He had been to school for just about two years!

So by the age of eleven Benjamin was employed in his father's business. And he didn't like it: 'I was employed in cutting wick for the candles, filling the dipping mold and the molds for cast candles, attending the shop, going on errands, etc. . . . I disliked the trade, and had a strong inclination for the sea.' As you can see from the picture, Boston was not then the big city it is today, so we can imagine Benjamin going on his errands round the little town with its rather muddy streets, and talking to its sober citizens.

The family decided that Benjamin needed a different sort of job. His brother James, nine years older than Benjamin, had just become a master printer and Benjamin went to be one of his apprentices to learn the printer's craft. Here was a real opportunity for a boy who loved books and reading of all kinds. He didn't have very much money, but he managed to buy or borrow all sorts of books. He also began to practise writing himself.

He had little time to read but he got up early and went to bed late to find some extra time. He even skipped church on Sundays, though his father would have disapproved very much of that.

Benjamin's apprenticeship to his brother did not work very well. They often quarrelled, but Benjamin stuck it out until he was seventeen. Then he decided he must leave Boston and try to earn a living somewhere else. He needed money so he sold some of his precious books and took a boat to New York to find work there with a man called William Bradford. Bradford could not offer him a job but suggested that he go to the Quaker city of

Philadelphia in Pennsylvania, to his son Andrew. Benjamin set off again. It was a long journey - there were no trains or aeroplanes then - and Benjamin went by boat and on foot. He arrived tired, hungry and dirty. He still had just enough money to buy some bread, and then he went into the Philadelphia Meeting House and fell fast asleep.

He did find work, not with Andrew Bradford, but with another printer, and gradually made friends in Philadelphia. One of them was no less a person than the governor of the province, Sir William Keith. Sir William suggested to him that he should go to England to set up his own printing business. He promised to help him by introducing him to English friends and lending him money. Benjamin thought it sounded like a wonderful opportunity and sailed to England full of hopes. But the governor's promises came to nothing and poor Benjamin had to find lodgings and work in a strange country. He stayed nineteen months before returning to Philadelphia - and he had to borrow £10 to help pay for his passage home.

Benjamin had learned a hard lesson, and he determined to be successful in business in his own country.

Philadelphia was the most thriving city in North America. Benjamin worked hard and within a few years became the most successful printer and publisher in the city. He was only 24. He felt he could afford a wife and family and he married a woman called Deborah Read. They lived happily together until she died 44 years later, and had a son and a daughter called Francis and Sarah.

Franklin's friends were also tradesmen: silversmiths, shoemakers, glaziers. They formed a society called the Junto or the Club of Leather Aprons. At their meetings they discussed many things but often they talked about how to improve the city. They lent each other books, and from this grew the idea of setting up a circulating library. They ordered books from London, and soon more people wanted to join in. The idea was copied in other American cities.

Benjamin himself had not lost his love of learning and books and taught himself to read French, Spanish, Italian and Latin. He published a kind of newspaper which he called *Poor Richard*. It was enormously popular and filled with improving mottoes and amusing sayings. A typical one was 'Three may keep a secret if two of them are dead'. So many people enjoyed reading *Poor Richard* that he was soon selling 10000 copies a year. He went on publishing it for 24 years.

Over the years Franklin and his friends helped to set up a police force, a fire brigade and a hospital. They made plans for improving street lighting and paving. They founded a college which later became the University of Pennsylvania.

He earned so much money in his business that by the time he was 42 he was able to leave the supervision of the work to others so that he could devote himself to the things he really longed to do.

Science was his great interest. Nowadays most scientists specialise in a particular branch of science, but in Franklin's lifetime very many fewer facts were known and it was possible for one man to study many areas of science.

Franklin studied earthquakes, waterspouts, thunderstorms, plants and animals. He investigated various illnesses and wrote about cures for kidney stones and cancer. He invented a stove which produced a current of warm air which circulated into the room; it was based on the principle of convection. He called it the Pennsylvania fireplace.

But it was through his work on electricity that Benjamin first became known outside America.

We are so used to electricity that it is quite difficult for us to think of the days before it was a common source of power. Try to think of a world without electric light, without radio, without television. No electric irons, no power plugs for washing machines and vacuum cleaners. All these things and many more have become possible through our understanding of electricity. But Franklin was working on electricity when very little was known about it.

In the course of his experiments Benjamin noticed that some materials attracted electricity and some repelled it. He wrote that 'bodies may be electrised *positively* or *negatively*. Or rather they may be electrised *plus* or *minus*'.

He noted that a person standing on wax was affected by electricity in a different way from someone standing on the floor. Wax is a non-conductor of electricity.

Benjamin wrote about his work to a friend in London called Peter Collinson. Collinson published the letters, with all their new ideas and discoveries, in a magazine and in a scientific journal. In 1751 all the letters were published together in a book called *Experiments and Observations on Electricity, made at Philadelphia in America.* Many people wanted to read it and it was translated into French, German and Italian. So it was that Franklin became known in Europe as a scientist. He often corresponded with scientists in different European countries.

This picture shows what is probably Benjamin's most famous experiment. For a long time he had been interested in meteorology, perhaps because he printed weather forecasts in *Poor Richard*. Several scientists of the time had already realised that lightning was electricity, but Franklin was probably the first to suggest how it could be proved by experiment.

Machines had already been made which would generate very small amounts of electricity. In one, for example, you turned a handle and a silk pad was rubbed against a glass drum. The glass became electrified and would attract light objects like pieces of paper or hair. It was also known that if you attached a piece of damp string to the glass drum, electricity would travel along the string and produce sparks at the other end.

Thinking over all these facts, Benjamin wondered if it would be possible to bring down to earth electricity from the lightning in the sky. He knew that metal attracted electricity and it occurred to him that if he could fly a silk kite with a metal rod attached to it during a thunderstorm, the electricity might run down the string dampened by the rain. If he tied a metal key to the end of the string he was holding, the metal would produce sparks and show that electricity was present.

Today we know that this experiment was dreadfully dangerous. The electrical forces in a thunderstorm are enormously powerful and Benjamin might easily have been killed. However, his luck held. He flew his kite in a dramatic thunderstorm and after a few false starts he felt the key prickling in his hands. Electricity from the skies!

The practical Benjamin realised how useful this piece of scientific knowledge was. It could prevent high buildings being damaged by lightning. If you fixed a piece of metal to the side of a building so that it stuck up at the top and so that the bottom was buried in the earth, the lightning would strike the metal and run down it safely to the earth. The lightning conductor was born.

Benjamin refused to patent his invention. He thought that everyone should benefit from it, and he did not want to profit from it personally.

So now Benjamin was a succesful business man, a well-known journalist, and a famous scientist. He was also a member both of the Philadelphia town council and of the governing body of Pennsylvania. And he had only been to school for two years!

At that time America was part of the British Empire, and the British parliament made laws for it. But the Americans felt that they ought to have more say in their own affairs. In particular they thought that the British parliament ought not to tax them without their consent. They twice sent Franklin to England to argue their case for them.

For many years he succeeded in helping the Americans and the English to understand each other, and solved many problems. He seemed a very ordinary figure in his plain clothes and old-fashioned wig. Many of the fashionable ladies and gentlemen of London must have thought him very provincial, but he was of course a famous scientist and thinker, and his house in London was often filled with the many friends and visitors who wanted to meet him.

In the end, however, even Benjamin could not reconcile the English and American ideas and the Americans decided that it was worth fighting for complete independence from Britain. In 1776 - by now Franklin was an old man of 70 - the Americans approved their Declaration of Independence.

They knew that Britain would not give in without a struggle, and that they would have to fight a hard war. Benjamin said, 'Gentlemen, we must now all hang together, or we shall most assuredly hang separately!' Just the sort of thing he might have printed in *Poor Richard.*

At first the war did not go well for the Americans, and Franklin agreed - a little reluctantly for he felt he might be too old - to go to France to seek help from the French government.

He was already well known in France through his scientific work, and he became extremely popular there. (There was even a hairstyle called the Franklin hairstyle!) He needed all his tact and popularity, for it was difficult to persuade the French to support the Americans. In the end, however, they did send weapons, soldiers and ships. The British found it impossible to win a war being fought three thousand miles from home, and in 1783 they were forced to recognise the American states as 'free, sovereign and independent'.

Benjamin stayed on in France for another two years as the representative of his newly independent country.

While in France he continued with his scientific work and in 1783 he saw the first two men go up in a free balloon. Their names were Pilatre de Rozier and the Marquis d'Arlandes.

What would he have thought of the first men to go up in a rocket to the moon? The first balloonists were French, but the first men on the moon were Franklin's own countrymen.

Benjamin immediately realised that the balloon could be used as a weapon in the war. He thought that if balloons could be sent over enemy territory, countries would think that war was useless, since no country would be able to protect itself properly. That was an optimistic idea which did not come true!

While he was still in France he wrote a book to describe America to the Europeans. It was called *Information to Those Who Would Remove to America.* We have to remember that in those days it took many weeks to sail to America and comparatively few people went there. It must have seemed very remote to people living in Europe. Benjamin described it as a country full of opportunities for craftsmen and farmers.

Franklin was now a very old man, and he wanted to return to his own country. He had several times reminded the American government that he had been away from home for years, but they had always persuaded him to stay in Europe and continue trying to make treaties between America and the various European countries.

In 1785 - when he was 79 - Benjamin did return to his own country. He was old and ill and the king of France sent him from Paris to the coast in a royal litter carried by mules.

On the long voyage home he wrote a pamphlet called *The Causes and Cure of Smokey Chimneys,* and he also took samples of the sea-water.

He showed that if ships carried thermometers they could test the temperature of the water, and so find the Gulf Stream, which is warmer than the surrounding water. By finding out where it was they could avoid its current, which is strong enough to slow down ships. So even his last voyage was not wasted.

When his boat at last arrived in Philadelphia, all the citizens turned out to welcome him. Did he think of the day, 62 years before, when he had first arrived there, tired, hungry and poor?

Even though he was so old, he was invited to become president of the supreme executive council of Pennsylvania. He often told the council stories about his long life, and it is said that when he left the council chamber the vice-president used sometimes to say, 'Come, gentlemen, it is time to proceed to business now that the president is gone.'

This picture of the Eiffel Tower in Paris shows the lightning conductor on the top. It is for this invention that Franklin is often remembered today, though of course it was just a small part of his work.

He was the man who foresaw, perhaps more clearly than anybody else at the time, that America would become a powerful country. In 1770 he wrote: 'America, an immense territory, favoured by nature with all the advantages of climate, soil, great navigable rivers, and lakes, etc. must become a great country, populous and mighty'.

Benjamin died when he was 84, and a crowd of 20 000 people came to his funeral. Long before, when he was a young man, he had written a mock epitaph for himself:

The body of
B. Franklin Printer
(Like the Cover of an Old Book
Its Contents torn out
And stript of its Lettering and Gilding)
Lies here, Food for Worms.
But the Work shall not be lost;
For it will, (as he believ'd) appear once more,
In a new and more elegant Edition
Revised and corrected
By the Author.

Granada Publishing Limited
English Language edition: Copyright © 1977 by Hart-Davis Educational Ltd
Frogmore, St Albans, Herts
and
3 Upper James Street, London, W1 4BP

Copyright © original edition and all other rights by
I.P.A. International Publishers' Aid, Bruges, Belgium

Translated and adapted for the English edition by Patricia Green

ISBN 0 247 12805 8